THE WHALE SCIENTISTS

Solving the Mystery of Whale Strandings

www.houghtonmifflinbooks.com

The text of this book is set in Perpetua.

Library of Congress Cataloging-in-Publication Data
Hodgkins, Fran, 1964 –
  The whale scientists: solving the mystery of whale strandings / by Fran Hodgkins.
    p. cm.
  Includes index.
  ISBN-13: 978-0-618-55673-1 (hardcover)
  ISBN-10: 0-618-55673-7 (hardcover)
  1. Whales—Juvenile literature. 2. Whaling—Juvenile literature. 3. Whales—Stranding—Juvenile literature. I. Title.
  QL737.C4H626 2007
  599.5—dc22   2006034634

Printed in Singapore
TWP 10 9 8 7 6 5 4 3 2 1

Illustration Credits

Page 6, illustration: Carl Buell
Page 7, illustration: Carl Buell, from http://www.neoucom.edu/Depts/Anat/Thewissen/whale_origins/whales/Pakicetid.html
Page 8 (top), photo: © David Pruter/Dreamstime.com; (bottom): National Oceanic and Atmospheric Administration Central Library Photo Collection
Pages 10 and 11, photos: Edward S. Curtis Collection, Library of Congress
Page 12, illustration: Will Hester/Sasha Blanton
Page 13, photo: Jeffrey Lepore/Photo Researchers, Inc.
Page 14, illustrations: National Oceanic and Atmospheric Administration Central Library Photo Collection
Page 15, photo: Rachel L. Sellers/Shutterstock
Page 16, photo: Chris Overgaard/iStockphoto
Page 17, photo: Garrett Nudd/iStockphoto
Page 18, photo: Iain Kerr Ocean Alliance
Page 19, photo: © Greenpeace/Rex Weyler
Page 20, photo: Ralph Lee Hopkins/Photo Researchers, Inc.
Page 21, photo: Peter Gordon/Shutterstock

Page 22, photo: Jupiterimages.com
Page 24, photo: Arnold Miller/Cape Cod Times
Page 25, photo: Tomasz Gulla/Shutterstock
Page 26, photo: Nikk Anderson/iStockphoto
Page 27, illustration: Katherine Zecca
Page 28, illustration: Stephanie Cooper
Page 29, image: Gary A. Glatzmeyer
Page 30, photo: John Makely/Baltimore Sun
Page 31, photo: Francois Gothier/Photo Researchers, Inc.
Page 32 (top), photo: Keith Chandler, Seaside Aquarium; (bottom) CDC/courtesy of Cynthia S. Goldsmith; William Bellini, Ph.D.
Page 33, photo: Kenn Kiser/stock.xchng.com
Page 35, photo: Arnold Miller/Cape Cod Times
Page 36, photo: Mark Newman/Photo Researchers, Inc.
Page 38, photo: Jeffrey Greenberg/photo Researchers, Inc.
Page 39 (top and bottom) and page 40 (top), photo: courtesy of the Maryland Department of Natural Resources, www.dnr.maryland.gov
Page 40 (bottom), photo: Carsten Medom Madsen/Shutterstock
Page 41, photo: U.S. Department of Commerce, National Institute of Standards and Technology (NIST)
Page 42 (top), photo: James Di Loreto; (bottom): Dr. Dani Kerem
Page 43, photo: Woods Hole Oceanographic Institution
Page 45, photo: Don Kenny
Page 47, photo: Cape Cod Stranding Network
Pages 48 and 49, photo: Arnold Miller/Cape Cod Times
Pages 50 and 51, photo: Mystic Aquarium
Page 52, illustration: Will Hester/Sasha Blanton
Page 53, photo: National Oceanic and Atmospheric Administration Central Library Photo Collection
Page 54, photo: sethakan/iStockphoto.com
Page 56, cartoon: Geoff Hook

To Sister Theresa Pond, with love and thanks for all your encouragement and for the faith you've had in me over the years.
—F. H.

THE WHALE SCIENTISTS

Solving the Mystery of Whale Strandings

by Fran Hodgkins

HOUGHTON MIFFLIN COMPANY
BOSTON 2007

Contents

CHAPTER THREE

Getting Answers from Strandings

page 37

CHAPTER FOUR

A Tragedy and a Triumph

page 47

Like a modern crocodile, Ambulocetus (am-bew-lo-see-tus) — whose name means "walking whale"— may have hunted about 49 million years ago by ambushing animals that came to the water's edge to drink.

A TRANSFORMED MAMMAL

Among the mammals—the animals that have hair and that feed their young milk—there is no mistaking a whale for anything but a whale. With their streamlined shape, lack of hind limbs, up-and-down tail motion, and almost completely hairless skin, whales are standouts in the animal kingdom. Called different names depending on their size—whale, dolphin, porpoise—they live their entire lives in the sea.

They didn't always.

About 55 million years ago, whales looked more like wolves than whales. They had sharp teeth and hoofed toes and noses at the ends of their snouts. One of several kinds of early whales was *Pakicetus* (pak-e-see-tuss), which was about the size of a dog. Its fossils are found mostly in Pakistan, near the sites of ancient rivers. *Pakicetus* may have looked for animals to eat near riverbanks or in the water. Time passed and the whales' ancestors changed; one, *Ambulocetus,* has been described as a "furry crocodile"—not only for its appearance but also for the way it hunted. Like a modern croc, *Ambulocetus* probably hid in the water, only its eyes and nostrils visible. When another animal came to drink—*wham!*—*Ambulocetus* grabbed its prey and dragged it under.

Pakicetus, *an early ancestor of whales and dolphins, lived in what is now Asia about 55 million years ago.*

7

The orca, shown here, catches fish and seals with its many sharp teeth. It is a member of the odontocetes, the toothed whales.

The humpback whale is a baleen whale: instead of teeth, its upper jaw is fringed with plates of baleen. Strong and flexible, the baleen works as a sieve, holding in fish and allowing water to pass out.

Over the next 30 million years, whales gave up their ties to the land altogether. Scientists think that living in the water gave the whales better access to food, such as fish, that land-based predators couldn't catch as easily. Their fur, which made swimming slow, gradually fell away as the millennia passed; its job of insulating the body was taken over by a layer of fat, or blubber, beneath the skin. Their hind legs shriveled, eventually shrinking to small bones inside their bodies. Their tails developed boneless flukes that drove them swiftly through the water. Their forelegs shortened, and the bones of the forefoot became the bones of a flipper. Their bodies, freed by the supportive nature of the water, grew larger than would have been possible on land.

Paleontologist Hans Thewissen, who discovered *Ambulocetus,* says, "Whales underwent the most dramatic and complete transformation of any mammal." Since the 1990s, many new fossil whales have been found in Asia, giving scientists a much more complete picture of how a four-legged animal moved into the ocean.

By the mid-Eocene period (about 37 million years ago), five major groups of cetaceans (see-tay-shuns) ruled the sea. (Scientists call whales and their relatives cetaceans, much as dogs, bears, and tigers are called carnivores and humans, apes, and monkeys are primates.) Today, there are two major groups: the toothed whales, or odontocetes (oh-don't-oh-seets), which include dolphins, porpoises, and the giant sperm whale, and the baleen whales, or mysticetes (miss-ti-seets), which include the bowhead, the humpback, and the largest animal ever, the blue whale. With their sharp-teethed jaws, the odontocetes eat meat, including seals, in the case of orcas. The mysticetes do not have teeth; instead, sheets of flexible tissue, called baleen, hang from their upper jaw. When a baleen whale eats, it opens its mouth and takes in thousands of gallons of water along with any fish, krill, or other small sea creatures the water contains. Next, the whale pushes the

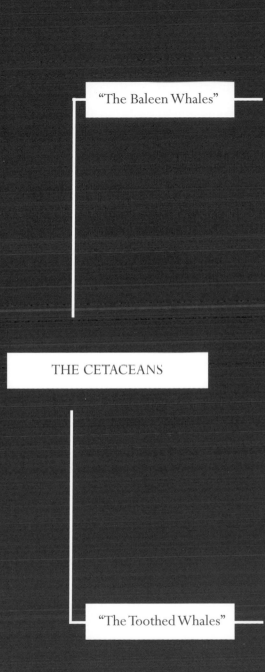

"The Baleen Whales"	Balaenopteridae	The humpback whale and rorquals — the blue whale, fin whale, sei whale, Bryde's whale, and minke whale
	Balanidae	The bowhead whale, Northern right whale, Southern right whale
	Neobalaenidae	The pygmy right whale
	Eschrichtidae	The gray whale
THE CETACEANS	Delphinidae	33 species, including the orca, pilot whale, bottlenose dolphin, and spinner dolphin
	Physeteridae	The sperm whale
	Kogiidae	The dwarf sperm whale and the pygmy sperm whale
	Phocoenidae	6 species, including the harbor porpoise
	Ziphiidae	21 species, including Hector's beaked whale and Perrin's beaked whale
	Monodontidae	The beluga and the narwhal
"The Toothed Whales"	Iniidae	The boto
	Pontoporiidae	The franciscana and the baiji (believed extinct in 2006)
	Platanistidae	The Ganges susu and Indus susu

Modern whales can be divided into two groups: the toothed whales, which include porpoises, dolphins, and the sperm whale; and the baleen whales, which include the humpback, blue, and bowhead whales.

Whale meat dries in the sun on a rack in the Inuit village at Hooper Bay, Alaska, circa 1929.

Inuit women butcher a beluga at Kotzebue, Alaska, circa 1929. The smaller whales, the beluga and the narwhal, were important to the survival of the Inuit.

water out through the baleen, trapping the prey, and finally swallows its meal.

Toothed whales and baleen whales share a mystery: sometimes they come ashore, or strand. They may strand singly or by the hundreds. When on land, their bodies suffer incredible damage from the sun, lack of water, and even their own weight. Why would an animal do something that will most likely cause it to die? Around the world, scientists are trying to find the answer.

First encounters

Although there's no way to know for sure, a stranded whale may have been the first whale a human had ever seen. Ancient people surely would have taken advantage of this bounty from the sea, whether it was the body of a small harbor porpoise or a giant sperm whale. When humans set to sea, the curious cetaceans probably swam up to investigate the boats, which they had never seen before. Besides learning how to catch fish, humans learned to catch the curious whales as well. One method was to maneuver boats around a herd, or pod, of whales and drive them into shore, where people killed them with spears.

Other people, such as the Inuit, rowed out to the whale and struck it with harpoons. The harpoon, unlike the spear, had a barbed end that would not pull out of the whale's body. Skin ropes attached the harpoons to sealskin floats; the floats hampered the whale's efforts to get away, gave away the whale's location, and slowed it down. There is evidence that the Inuit hunted whales as many as five thousand years ago, pursuing the small white beluga, the narwhal, and the bowhead, the great whale they called *Aghvook* or *Agviq*.

Early whale hunters stayed near shore. Around A.D. 900, ship technology advanced and larger vessels set out to sea. One of the first oceangoing peoples, the Vikings of Scandinavia, hopscotched across the Atlantic by sailing from Norway to

Inuit men of Cape Prince of Wales, Alaska, launch their umiak to pursue a bowhead whale. Their methods were similar to those of their ancestors. Each whale would be divided among the crew and the villagers. This photograph was taken in 1929, but Inuit whaling methods remain much the same today.

Britain, to Iceland, to Greenland, and then on to North America. Along the way, they learned to hunt whales with barbed metal harpoons, like the one pictured here.

Whaling for profit begins

Whaling changed around the end of the ninth century, when the Basque people became whale hunters. The Basques lived on the Bay of Biscay, which washes the coasts of Spain and France. Every year, whales came to the bay and the Basques set to sea to get them. They ate the meat, burned the oil in lamps, made the bones into furniture, and even found uses for the baleen, including shredding it into helmet crests. Basque salesmen traveled Europe to find buyers for whale products and found many takers. Whaling for profit had begun.

Some experts think the Basques learned how to whale from the Vikings. Whoever taught them, they quickly became the experts. They hunted the right whale, a large, slow-moving baleen whale that floated when it was dead. In the 1500s, their search for whales took them across the Atlantic to Red Bay, Labrador, where they set up the first commercial whale-processing site in North America. Red Bay lies on the Strait of Belle Isle, which was a major migration route for right whales during the summer and bowheads during the fall. In fifty years, the Basques killed twenty thousand whales, effectively wiping out the whale populations that migrated through the strait. Even today, about five hundred years later, whales do not travel the Strait of Belle Isle.

The money to be made from whaling drew other nations to it. The English started whaling (usually hiring Basque whalers to help), but they were not very good at it, and soon the Dutch took over. The Dutch were efficient whalers and very good businessmen. They hunted whales off Iceland, Greenland, and Spitsbergen, part of a group of islands called Svalbard in the Arctic Ocean north of Norway, where they established a large whale-processing site called Smeerenberg, literally

Now abandoned, shore stations such as this one at Leith Harbor on South Georgia Island in the South Atlantic Ocean, served as bases for whalers for many years. The whales would be killed at sea and then towed to shore, where they would be cut up and their tissues boiled down for oil. Rusty now, the storage tanks once held hundreds of barrels of whale oil.

At sea, whalers drew the dead whale alongside to begin the slaughtering process, called "cutting in."

To get at the valuable oil inside a sperm whale's head, whalers would cut off the whale's head and use a bucket to "bail in the case."

"Blubbertown." The Americans, too, got into the whaling business, even before the United States became an independent nation.

Like the Basques before them, these whalers mostly wanted whale oil. All the whale's body tissues are rich in fatty oil. Oil was valuable for lighting (it wouldn't be until 1883 that Thomas Edison patented the electric light bulb), as well as for lubricating machinery, heating, and making cosmetics and soap.

All the activities associated with whaling — stripping, boiling, and sealing the oil in barrels — were now done at sea. A dead whale was stripped of its oil-rich blubber, which was then tried, or boiled in huge vats. Because the meat usually spoiled before it could be eaten, it was also boiled down for its oil. The great vats were set on the ship's deck in a brick firebox, or fuel-burning chamber, called the tryworks. The oil came out of the tissues and rose to the top. When cool, it was skimmed off, sealed in barrels (each holding more than three hundred gallons), and taken back to the mainland for sale.

At the time, so the story goes, an American whaling captain killed the first sperm whale and discovered that this whale offered the businessman a new opportunity: the candle business.

In the 1700s, people used candles to light their homes. Some candles were made from beeswax, but only the wealthy could afford them. Most people made do with cheaper tallow candles, which were smoky and smelly. The whalers discovered that a sperm whale's great square head contains a huge capsule, called the case. The case is filled with oil—seventy-five to ninety barrels' worth in a large male—and a waxy substance called spermaceti. Spermaceti could be used to make candles that did not smoke (or stink) when burned and were more affordable than beeswax. To get the oil and spermaceti, the whalers would cut off the whale's head after killing it and use a bucket to empty the case, a process called "bailing in the case."

The whalers also took the baleen from the whales' mouths. Strong and flexible, baleen was used for many things that we use plastic for today, such as umbrella ribs, brushes, and brooms. Its popularity soared in the 1800s when the wasp waist and large hoop skirts became fashionable. Women strapped themselves into baleen ("whalebone") corsets, which compressed their bodies and shrank their waists to about eighteen inches in circumference. In 1853, more than 5.5 million pounds of baleen came to America, taken from the mouths of hundreds of thousands of slaughtered whales.

American, Basque, Dutch, and English whalers all hunted whales in much the same way. Human muscle propelled sleek rowboats to a sighted whale, human muscle killed the whale, and human muscle towed the dead whale back to the sail-powered whaleship. Although the whalers took thousands of whales and did considerable damage, the swift rorquals (the baleen whales with pleated throats, including blue, fin, sei, Bryde's, and minke whales) escaped—they simply swam too fast for the whalers to catch.

That was about to change.

Industrial whaling reigns

In the late 1800s whaling technology changed tremendously. First came the steam engine and the steamship. Propelled by a powerful engine instead of the wind, steamships outpaced even the fastest sailing ships. In a steam-driven whaleship, whalers captured and killed all kinds of whales, even the fleet rorquals.

Next, the harpoon changed. Svend Føyn of Norway developed one that carried an explosive charge. When the harpoon entered the whale, the charge exploded, ripping up the animal's internal organs and immediately

A mother and her daughter pose for a formal photograph in the early 1900s. The daughter's fashionably tiny waist resulted from being confined by a whalebone corset, an undergarment that contained strips of baleen. Many women fainted and many whales died for this look.

In the twentieth century, whaling ships fired explosive harpoons from cannonlike guns that were positioned on their bows.

crippling it. Føyn's invention ended the long "Nantucket sleigh rides" whalers had endured after harpooning a whale that would not die quickly.

Modern whaling had begun.

Between 1900 and 1940, whalers killed 794,000 whales. It is not recorded how many wounded whales escaped to die elsewhere. Despite annual agreements limiting the number of whales to be killed, the whales were in serious decline, and the whaling nations began to realize that. Humpbacks had been essentially wiped out by 1915, and blues by 1936. So whalers formed the International Whaling Commission (IWC) as a governing body in 1946. The IWC set a time during the year when whales could be hunted (December 15–April 1) and devised a program of "blue whale units": the blue, being the largest whale, gave the most oil, and so the system allowed whalers to kill several smaller whales to "equal" one blue whale. The IWC also established quotas that limited how many whales could be killed, and length minimums, which were meant to protect young whales from being killed.

During the mid- and late twentieth century, whaling was conducted with military precision. Small planes and, later, helicopters spotted the whales and radioed their location to killer ships. Armed with cannon-fired harpoons, the ships chased and killed the whales, leaving the bodies marked with floats. Tuglike boats towed the bodies to the factory ship, the centerpiece of the whaling fleet. The factory ship dragged the whale aboard through a ramp in the stern and reduced it to nothing but a few scraps in less than an hour. It was all extremely efficient.

So efficient that many whales were nearly wiped out. About 350,000 blue whales died during the time of the hunters; today, between 400 and 1,400 remain, according to IWC estimates. The gray whale suffered huge losses, too:

of the three populations that once existed (Eastern North Pacific, Western North Pacific, and Atlantic), the Atlantic is completely gone, and the Western North Pacific is practically extinct, now down to about 100 whales. The North Atlantic right whale is also nearly extinct, with about 350 animals left.

Fortunately for the whales, another change was on the horizon.

Learning more about cetaceans

Psychologists have long recognized that people find it easy to kill things they fear or don't understand. In the eighteenth and nineteenth centuries, and even into the twentieth, many people saw whales as nothing other than murderous monsters. Artists and writers depicted them as vicious creatures, especially in pictures of whales vengefully smashing whaleboats. Whales that stranded themselves on shore were occasions for photograph taking, sometimes with people standing on top of the dying animals. Whales were things to be conquered and vanquished.

In 1938, knowledge about whales began to spread, for that year Marine Studios (now Marineland) in Florida put bottlenose dolphins on display. After World War II, other facilities did too.

The people who ran those facilities encouraged researchers to come and study their cetaceans. Among those researchers was psychologist John C. Lilly, who studied dolphins. Their intelligence intrigued him, and Dr. Lilly devoted the rest of his life to studying and writing popular books about dolphins. He hoped that dolphins and humans would one day learn to communicate.

While Lilly explored the mystical side of cetaceans, oceanographer and inventor Jacques Cousteau was bringing the ocean into people's living rooms. He and his crew journeyed the world aboard the *Calypso,* studying the sea and its creatures and making films that showed animals, including cetaceans, in their natural habitats.

A young human and a bottlenose dolphin size each other up at an aquarium. Before 1938, seeing a dolphin or any other cetacean face-to-face was impossible; once Marine Studios put bottlenose dolphins on display, people began to enjoy and appreciate cetaceans.

In 1967, Roger Payne, shown, and Scott McVay discovered the elaborate songs sung by humpback whales, which are a form of communication.

In 1967, whale researchers Roger Payne and Scott McVay recorded the songs of humpback whales. Although some scientists scoffed at Payne's theory that whales used the songs for long-distance communication, the biologist was eventually proved right. Recordings of the songs have since sold millions of copies. Space scientists included humpback songs on a disk of Earth sounds that was attached to the *Voyager* spacecraft—the first human-made object to leave our solar system.

Seeing, reading about, and hearing whales helped people understand: These creatures were not monsters to be feared and slaughtered on principle. Many lived in family groups whose members helped one another (whalers had known this for years; they would wound one member of a herd to keep the others nearby). At least one species, the humpback, performed songs to communicate with others. Their intelligence seemed not so different from our own. These revelations came at a time when people — especially young people — were becoming more politically active and more concerned with the environment. It was only natural that whaling should become a target.

In 1971, a group of Americans had campaigned against nuclear testing in Canada. In the book *To Save a Whale: The Voyages of Greenpeace,* Robert Hunter and Rex Weyler recounted the following story: During their voyage to a remote Aleutian island to protest nuclear tests, the ship's captain had remarked, "Used to be, when you came out here on the Gulf, you could see them whales from horizon to horizon. . . . 'Course, you don't see them any longer. They're extinct." His words haunted Hunter and Weyler. Four years later, they led their group, Greenpeace, out into the Pacific to confront the whalers.

Greenpeace's actions drew international attention. The organization's volunteers tracked down whaleships and launched Zodiacs, rubber boats fitted

In the 1970s, Greenpeace drew public attention to whaling
activities by confronting the huge whaling ships, such as these
from the former Soviet Union, at sea. The group and others are
still working to protect whales.

Here's looking at you: The gray whale was one of the species listed as endangered by the United States, protecting it in American waters and helping it begin to recover; the Eastern Pacific gray whales are the most numerous of the three subgroups of the species.

with outboard motors. They maneuvered the Zodiacs between the whales and the harpoons. These actions not only allowed many whales to escape, but also captured the public imagination — photographs of a tiny, fragile rubber boat against an immense steel ship were difficult to ignore.

The United States placed eight of the great whale species found in American waters on its national endangered species list: the blue, humpback, fin, right, gray, bowhead, sei, and sperm whale; the smaller species, such as the minke, were more numerous than these eight. Under the Endangered Species Act of 1973, the U.S. government protects all listed animals; no one could hunt these whales within two hundred miles of the American coast. The Endangered Species Act and another law, the Marine Mammal Protection Act of 1972, made American waters a giant sanctuary for whales.

The United States pushed the IWC for stronger limits on whaling, too. Opposing these limits were Japan and the former Soviet Union. In 1986, the IWC instituted a "zero quota" on all commercial whaling — that is, no whales could be killed for humans or animals to eat except by members of certain groups who had traditionally hunted the whales, such as the Inuit. However, the quota system does allow countries to give special permits to kill whales for scientific research. Among the nations that have such permits are Japan, Norway, and Iceland. Despite pressure from other nations, whale meat still appears for sale in Japanese and Norwegian markets, and pirate whalers kill whales illegally. Some nations are demanding that the ban on commercial whaling be lifted, saying that the populations of whales have recovered enough to allow for whaling to begin again.

Determining whether it is "safe" to allow whaling to resume is complicated by our lack of knowledge about the lives of whales. The IWC acknowledges that for many species, not enough scientific information is available even to form the basis of a reliable population estimate. Like other large mammals, whales mature slowly and reproduce slowly. Females bear only one calf at a time, and pregnancy lasts for a year or more. The calf then depends on its mother for food for months longer, depending on the species. A female may have a calf once every two years, as with the blue whale, or once every five years, as with the sperm whale. Such a slow reproductive rate means that it will take many years for whales to reach their pre–industrial whaling populations.

Yet whales may now be more valuable to people alive than they are dead. Whale watching has become big business. Boats sail from both coasts of the United States and from many other nations. In 1998, more than 9 million people around the world went whale watching, spending more than a billion dollars on tickets and souvenirs.

After so many centuries of killing whales, we have only recently engaged in learning about them—including what makes them come ashore, which is where humans first encountered them so long ago.

Although Japan says it conducts whaling strictly for scientific research, this whale meat is for sale in a grocery store in Tokyo. Norway and Iceland still hunt whales for their meat as well. These nations argue that eating whale meat is part of their cultural heritage, although statistics show that the average person in Japan eats less than a single ounce of whale meat each year.

This whale stranded alone on a sandy beach. The question is, why?

WHY DO WHALES STRAND?

Every stranding is different. Sometimes the whales are alive; other times they have died at sea and washed ashore. Some strandings involve just one animal; others include one hundred or more whales. For some critically endangered species, such as the North Atlantic right whale, every stranded whale means that the species itself has taken another step toward extinction. As scientists struggle to make sense of these incidents, they have developed a number of theories as to why whales strand. Scientists around the world are constantly testing these theories, seeking evidence that will support or disprove them. In the end, whale scientists may find that there is no single cause.

Hearing damage

The ocean is a noisy place. Fish, invertebrates, and even the waves themselves are natural sources of sound in the ocean. Certain events can make the sea much louder—a thunderstorm or undersea earthquake—but they are short-lived and occur in relatively small areas. Scientists have learned that this constant background noise doesn't bother marine mammals. After millions of years in the ocean, they've gotten used to it—much like you may not really hear the sound of a fan that runs in your room at night. Because their bodies have adapted to this natural background noise, it does not harm their hearing.

Mass strandings involve groups of whales, such as these pilot whales. Rescuers covered them with wet towels to protect their skin from drying out.

So, the sea may be *naturally* noisy, but human activities are making it noisier.

Boats carry more than 90 percent of the products traded between countries, everything from cars to books to computers. These cargo ships generate noise with their engines and propellers as they move through the water, and the older the ship, the noisier it can be. Shipping routes are among the noisiest places in the sea. As trade increases, more ships will travel the sea. More ships means more noise.

Ships also use sonar to avoid undersea obstacles, to find schools of fish, and, in wartime, to search out enemy submarines. A ship emits a loud sound pulse that travels quickly through the water and bounces off any objects in the way — shoals of fish, undersea mountains, and submarines. Although sound travels faster in water than in air, it takes a lot of energy to make a sound travel far underwater; therefore, the sound must be very loud. According to the Natural Resources Defense Council, some kinds of sonar emit pulses louder than 235 decibels, similar to the launch of a space rocket.

In 2000, thirteen beaked whales, a spotted dolphin, and two minke whales stranded in the Bahamas. Some were rescued, but others died. Earlier in that same area, the United States Navy had conducted tests of a new kind of sonar that was more powerful than those of the past. Necropsies, which are examinations of an animal after it dies, showed that the whales' ears and brains had been bleeding before the animals died. Other strandings around the world have been connected to sonar tests, in regions such as the Pacific Northwest of the United States, the U.S. Virgin Islands, and the Canary Islands, and the area near Yokosuka, Japan.

In 2005, sonar tests were suspected to have contributed to a multiple-species stranding in North Carolina. Although the sonar tests and the stranding could not be directly linked, the event was similar to other noise-induced strandings in that

Carrying containers of manufactured products, a container ship steams into port. Each year, more ships like this make more trips across the oceans — adding their engine noises to the whales' already noisy environment.

the stranded whales were from different species (pilot whales and pygmy sperm whales), were alive when they stranded, and didn't share any diseases or other physical problems.

You may be thinking, wouldn't whales swim away if a loud noise bothered them? Believe it or not, not always. Near Newfoundland, Canada, a group of humpback whales didn't leave an area when undersea blasting began, although the sound was loud enough to hurt them. And bowhead whales return to the Beaufort Sea north of Alaska every year at the same time blasting goes on. Even whale-watching boats, with their noisy propellers and crowds of passengers, don't scare off whales once the whales get used to them.

Besides causing hearing damage, loud or intrusive sounds disrupt the rhythms of life. Imagine yourself on a particularly noisy occasion—say, a holiday with lots of talkative relatives. There's music, maybe, and a football game playing on the TV. When everybody leaves, you probably feel worn out. That's because the hubbub added stress to your system. Even if you were enjoying yourself, your body reacted to the heightened noise level—that is, it was stressed.

Being exposed to stress over a long period of time can make you sick; for example, students often fall ill during vacation after a week full of exams. Does the same thing happen to cetaceans? There hasn't been enough research to say yes or no. However, whale researcher William Watkins found that excessive sound does affect the everyday interactions of whales by interrupting the normal conversations of humpbacks, sperm whales, right whales, bowheads, and pilot whales. It may very well add to stress and contribute to strandings.

Confusing geography

Toothed whales use their own natural sonar, called echolocation. In echolocation, toothed whales make high-pitched sounds. The sounds travel through the water

Once whales get used to the sound, noisy whale-watch boats like this one do not frighten whales away.

26

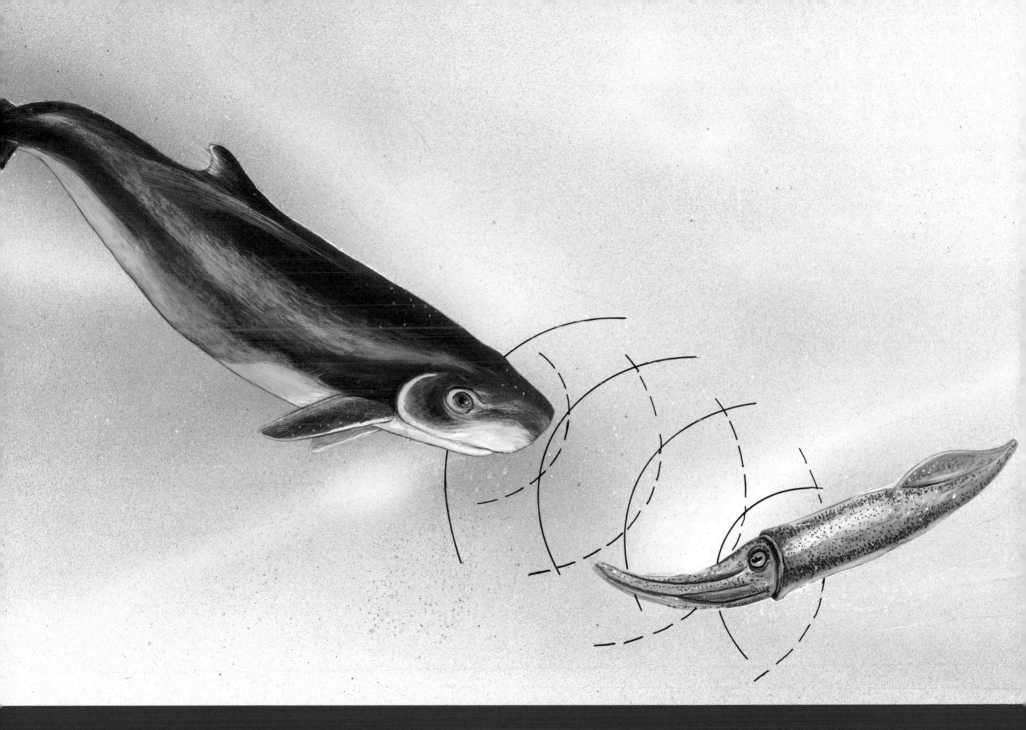

Toothed whales, such as this pygmy sperm whale, create sounds that travel through the water, strike objects (such as the squid shown here), and bounce back. Called echolocation, this ability allows whales to find prey and avoid obstacles even in dark water.

and bounce off anything in the way. The echo goes back to the whale and gives it a mental map of its surroundings. Echolocation helps whales find their way in dark water, and also helps them zero in on food.

In shallow water, the sounds bounce off not only obstacles, but also the sea bottom and the underside of the water's surface. Think of a room full of mirrors; each mirror reflects the image reflected off every other mirror, until eventually there are so many reflections that you can't make any sense of what you're seeing. For some toothed whales, making sense of many echolocation signals in shallow water may be just as confusing as finding your way out of a room full of mirrors.

Whale species that are used to deep water may get even more confused. Accustomed to having thousands of meters of water below them, a whale might misunderstand its own signals as they bounce back to it from the bottom, and turn toward the shallows rather than away from them. Unable to swim in such little water, the whale is trapped.

Cape Farewell in New Zealand and Cape Cod in Massachusetts are both whale traps. "The tides and currents, 'hooks' of land that jut out into the sea, gently sloping beaches, and shallow water make these areas especially hazardous for oceanic whales," says Sheryl Gibney of Project Jonah, a whale rescue program in New Zealand.

Magnetic attractions

Other scientists think that magnetism is to blame for whale strandings. A magnetic field surrounds the planet Earth, generated by its iron-rich core. Evidence is mounting that cetaceans and other marine animals can sense the field and use it to navigate. Researchers have found tiny amounts of a magnetic mineral in the brains of some species of animals, although not yet in whales. The mineral acts

CAPE COD

SCOTLAND

TASMANIA   NEW ZEALAND

as a natural internal compass, allowing the animal to detect the invisible lines of magnetism generated by Earth's magnetic field. Fish, rays, and sea turtles all have been tested in the lab; when researchers placed magnets on them, they struggled to orient themselves in their tanks.

Because cetaceans are large and difficult to experiment with, most evidence about how they navigate has come from analyzing stranding records. During the 1980s, biologist Margaret Klinowska of the University of Cambridge in England studied more than three thousand records. She found a relationship between the places cetaceans stranded and concentrations of iron-rich rock. She theorized that the iron-rich rocks disrupted the smooth pattern of magnetic fields that the whales followed, causing them to steer toward shore instead of away.

Marine scientist and physicist Klaus Vanselow of the University of Kiel in Germany studied records of strandings that occurred between 1712 and 2003. He found a connection between increased strandings and times when the sun is extra active, throwing plumes of hot gas hundreds of miles out from its surface. Such plumes, called solar flares, strike Earth's magnetic field, cause it to bend out of its normal shape, and even disrupt radio signals. Homing pigeons, which steer by the magnetic field, become disoriented when solar activity is high, and Vanselow thinks the same may be true for whales.

Weather

For decades, Tasmania has been the site of strandings of the largest toothed predator in the world, the sperm whale. In 2004, biologist Mark Hindell of the University of Tasmania and his graduate student Karen Evans discovered a connection between these strandings and the weather.

Evans and Hindell examined stranding records going back to the 1920s.

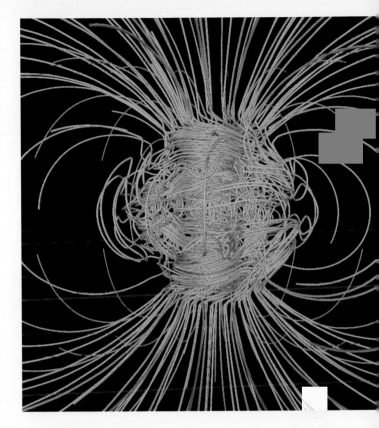

A map for whales: This computer model depicts Earth's magnetic field; the yellow strands indicate lines of magnetic force that are moving away from Earth, and the blue strands show the lines of magnetic force moving toward Earth. Some species of animals can sense the lines and use them to navigate.

They found that whales were more likely to strand when the weather was cold. "Strandings were thought to be pretty random events—or suspected of being linked to climate events like El Niño—but nothing had been demonstrated. We have shown a clear pattern," Dr. Hindell told *New Scientist*.

Hindell and Evans found that strandings increased every ten or twelve years. About every ten years, certain winds, called the zonal westerly winds, shift. Because wind patterns affect ocean waters, this shift increases the amount of cold, food-rich water that brushes the Tasmanian coast. Many whales and dolphins follow the food—and the cold water—toward shore, and end up stranded.

Whales and dolphins may also be stranded if a powerful storm hits. An early-winter storm on December 10, 2005, left fifteen pilot whales and twelve dolphins stranded on Cape Cod. Ninety-mile-an-hour winds whipped up the sea. None of the animals survived.

Charlie Potter of the Smithsonian Institution and Kevin Rosemary of the Maryland Department of Natural Resources measure the flukes of a sei whale that was found dead on the prow of a ship that entered Baltimore Harbor in April 2006. The whale was transported to a landfill for examination and burial.

Illness and injury

When researchers study stranded cetaceans, they often find evidence of illness and injuries, including broken bones, parasites, cuts, and ailments such as pneumonia.

At sea, whales and ships often run into each other, with serious results for the whales. Fortunate whales may escape such encounters with broken ribs or a few internal injuries that heal on their own. Less fortunate whales may die from their injuries after swimming away. Or, in a truly tragic encounter, the whale becomes trapped on the prow of the ship and dies, as was the case of a sei whale found dead when a cargo ship entered Baltimore Harbor in April 2006.

This pod of sperm whales was photographed off the Azore Islands in the North Atlantic Ocean. Some experts suspect that sperm whales may strand because of their close-knit family structure, while others have found evidence that the weather contributes to sperm whale strandings.

Parasites infect nearly all whales. A parasite is an animal that lives on or in another animal, taking nutrients from it and harming it. Many dolphins harbor a kind of parasite called a fluke in their nasal passages. Sometimes, the flukes leave the passages and work their way to the brain. There, they burrow in and lay their eggs, damaging and sometimes killing the brain. Other stranded whales have shown signs of parasites that have destroyed important nerves and affected the lungs, stomach, intestines, and liver.

In some cases, the parasites become a problem only after another illness weakens the animal's natural physical defenses,

Although scientists aren't sure exactly what caused this skinny gray whale to strand on the Oregon coast, it clearly could not find enough food to survive.

such as a disease caused by a bacterium or a virus. Many species of bacteria have been found during examinations of stranded whales, and most of them are harmful. Viruses, such as those of the genus *Morbillivirus,* have been found in cetaceans from around the world. Related to the measles virus, this one causes lesions in the brain, lymph nodes, digestive tract, and lungs.

In both 1999 and 2000, more than two hundred gray whales, alive and dead, were found stranded along the West Coast of the United States and Alaska, compared to the normal average of forty a year. Some seemed to be terribly thin. Although it may seem impossible, whales can starve, particularly when they cannot find the shoals of fish or clouds of krill they need to sustain themselves. Without food, the whale goes hungry, and may eventually strand and die, or die at sea. The reason for the 1999–2000 die-off of gray whales has never been fully explained.

It's very possible that sick or dying cetaceans strand themselves.

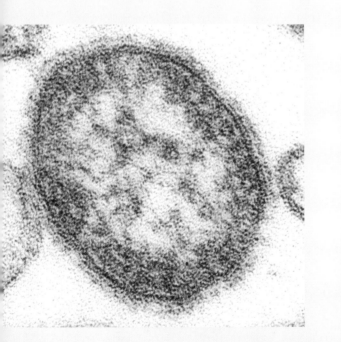

This is an electron micrograph of a morbillivirus that causes measles in humans; in whales, a morbillivirus causes injury to the brain, lungs, and other organs.

Toxins

Like dolphins and fish, ships move fastest when they are sleek and streamlined. A ship covered with barnacles is neither. Barnacles, which are related to lobsters and crabs, spend only part of their lives living free in the water. To grow to adulthood, a barnacle finds an anchoring spot—a ship's hull, a wharf piling, even a whale will do—and attaches itself. It then grows a shell similar to that of a clam. From the safety of its shell, the barnacle reaches out with its legs to grab whatever food is floating by. To remove the pesky critters, the ship must be taken out of the water and scraped clean—an expensive and time-consuming process. Barnacle problems cost international shipping millions of dollars each year.

That expense was cut down significantly when the chemical tributyltin (TBT) was added to ship paint. TBT kept barnacles from sticking to ships' hulls. No barnacles meant no hauling boats out of the water—and the more time a boat spent in the water, the more money could be made.

TBT had an unforeseen complication. Three researchers from the Yale University Medical School discovered that the chemical interfered with the workings of the hair cells inside the ears of all mammals. Located in the cochlea, a fluid-filled, spiral-shaped organ, the hair cells translate pressure changes of the fluid into electrical impulses that go to the brain. If the hair cells are damaged, the whale goes deaf. Unable to hear its echolocation sounds, a deaf toothed whale may strand.

Behavior

Although it isn't a direct cause of strandings, an aspect of cetacean behavior may lead to the deaths of many animals that might otherwise have lived.

Barnacles like these on a wharf piling encrust the hulls of ships, slowing their movement through the water. To keep ships sleek, their hulls are coated with a paint containing a chemical that keeps barnacles from sticking. But does the chemical harm whales' ears?

The species that mass strand most often—including the pilot whale and the sperm whale—are among the most social of all cetaceans. The pilot whale lives in large family groups of as many as ninety members. Sperm whales also live in large family groups, consisting mostly of females. Young males leave their families when they are between four and twenty-one years old to live in bachelor groups with other males. Researchers think that the whales may follow an ill family member to shore and as a result all of them strand.

Pilot and sperm whales are not alone in their family loyalty: in 1977, thirty false killer whales stranded on a beach in the Dry Tortugas, islands at the trailing end of the Florida Keys. Despite attempts to push them back into the sea, the whales would not leave a large male until he died, three days after the stranding. Loyalty has a high price for whales.

The ties that bind: Reluctance to leave a pod member who is ill or dying may contribute to strandings such as this one of pilot whales in Massachusetts.

Researchers scramble to get as much data as possible when they encounter a whale in the open sea such as this gray whale. Because of their size, their elusiveness, and the immensity of their environment, whales are possibly the most challenging to study of all nature's creatures.

GETTING ANSWERS FROM STRANDINGS

Scientists face huge obstacles as they try to find out the causes of whale strandings. Studying whales presents difficulties that other biologists don't have to deal with. A bug scientist can keep hundreds of specimens in a lab, because each creature needs only about as much room as a shoebox. Not only is a whale millions of times bigger than a bug, but it also needs a lot more living space. A scientist who wants to study larger animals, such as giraffes or polar bears, can find healthy specimens in many zoos. Aquariums seldom have whales on display. In the United States, only SeaWorld successfully keeps orcas, and the Mystic Aquarium in Connecticut and the Atlanta Aquarium are home to several belugas. Keeping cetaceans happy and healthy in captivity is not easy.

The difficulty in studying whales isn't limited to the lab. Land animals leave signs — tracks, tree rubbings, droppings, and burrows — that help scientists find them in the wild. Whale researchers are provided few clues. Instead, they have to go to where whales have been seen in the past and hope to see them again. Small wonder, then, that most of what we know about whales has come from stranded animals. Without closely studying these stranded animals, we would know much, much less about cetaceans than we do today.

In the United States, many stranded cetaceans that die are studied after death. Because the federal government protects all marine mammals, it requires

Researchers from the Marine Animal Rescue Society of Miami, Florida, examine a dead Cuvier's beaked whale on Miami Beach. An external examination is the first stage of an animal autopsy, or necropsy.

groups that respond to strandings to report on every stranded animal they deal with. Rescuers use one form for basic information and additional forms if the postmortem examination, or necropsy, is more involved—for example, if the stranded animal is an endangered North Atlantic right whale or if the animal dies after rehabilitation is attempted.

Dr. Cindy Driscoll of the Department of Veterinary Medicine of the University of Maryland conducts numerous necropsies each year. She and her staff bring small cetaceans, such as harbor porpoises, to the lab for study. Large animals need to be necropsied on the beach.

To get ready for a necropsy of a large whale, scientists need the following:

- Cutting tools, including scalpels, scalpel blades, and stainless steel and titanium knives of several lengths
- Rubber gloves
- Waterproof overalls and rubber boots (things get messy, and beach weather can be very cold and wet)
- Ziploc bags and glass bottles/jars for storing samples
- Goggles for going inside the whale or using a saw to cut large parts
- Turkey basters and syringes for collecting samples
- A GPS indicator to record the whale's position exactly
- Digital or film cameras and a video camera to record the necropsy
- Meat hooks
- Forceps
- Indelible ink pens, pencils, rulers and measuring tapes, and notepaper

Although some onlookers feel queasy during a necropsy, Dr. Driscoll says she doesn't really notice the gore factor. "You're always going to find something new, something that you haven't seen before, so you don't notice the unpleasantness," she explains.

Biologist Cindy Driscoll has conducted many necropsies during her career.

Biologists from the Maryland Department of Natural Resources conduct a necropsy on the sei whale that was found dead on the prow of a ship that entered Baltimore Harbor in April 2006. Blunt trauma was the cause of death; the whale suffered broken bones and internal bleeding.

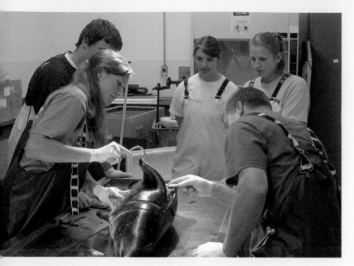

While large specimens must be necropsied outdoors, smaller cetaceans can be brought back to the laboratory for examination.

Fishing nets like this one are made to be invisible to the fish they capture, but they are also imperceptible to whales. If a net like this one tangles around a whale's jaws, it can prevent the whale from eating. Whale rescuers sometimes attempt to cut loose nets on whales at sea, but they don't always succeed.

First, researchers examine the skin, noting any wounds. The whale might have cuts from being hit by a boat or ship, bites from sharks, even gunshot wounds. Trained eyes look for clues to help determine whether these wounds were incurred when the whale was alive or after it died. Researchers also look for fishing line, plastic, or netting; some whales die because such materials entangle their jaws, keeping them from eating and leading to their death.

Researchers have to work quickly but carefully. Often, several teams work on different parts of the whale at the same time. Anyone who climbs on top of the whale must be careful not to fall, especially onto someone below who's got a large, sharp knife. Rainy weather can make the work difficult, but, as Dr. Driscoll explains, "from a deterioration perspective, the sun and heat are a lot harder for people." Because of its blubber, a whale's body doesn't release heat, and a dead whale on the beach will begin to literally cook from inside under the hot sun, destroying tissues and, with them, clues to what happened.

The whale's body openings, including the blowhole and esophagus, are examined for any signs of infection, or of contamination (such as sand or mud), and researchers use king-size cotton swabs to take samples of the mucus inside the openings; it will be analyzed for the presence of bacteria, viruses, and microscopic parasites. Researchers cut through the skin and the blubber beneath, which can be up to a foot thick, depending on the species of whale. They take three-centimeter-square samples of the liver, kidneys, heart, and all other major organs. Pathologists—scientists who specialize in diagnosing disease—will study those tissues, looking for chemicals, viruses, and other microorganisms.

Some of the samples go to the National Marine Mammal Tissue Bank in Gaithersburg, Maryland, and Charleston, South Carolina. The bank is run by the the National Institute of Standards and Technology (NIST) and the National Marine Fisheries service, the government agency that oversees cetaceans in the United

States. Frozen in liquid nitrogen, the samples are preserved for the long run.

Decades in the future, a scientist may compare a tissue sample from a whale that died in 2007 with the tissues of another whale to see how the ocean has changed. Certain animals, including the pilot whale, bowhead, and beluga, are called indicator species. Although these species are not critically endangered, they are used to judge the health of the oceans; if their tissues are contaminated with poisons or other pollutants, it can be a signal that the well-being of that entire ocean is at risk.

Sample sleuths

Although some kinds of whales are unmistakable — the sperm whale, with its head like a railroad boxcar, is a good example — others are more difficult to identify. The only way to identify a cetacean's species for certain is to analyze the DNA in its tissues. DNA (deoxyribonucleic acid) is a molecule present in nearly all living things that holds the blueprint of that organism. DNA is made up of units called bases; the arrangement of the bases is unique to every species, and to each individual within the species. By studying DNA, scientists can determine whether different species or individuals are related.

Just because two whales look alike doesn't mean they are the same species. Five whales stranded on the California coast between 1975 and 1997 were thought to be Hector's beaked whales. Beaked whales are generally shy, avoiding ships and researchers, and as a group are poorly understood. However, Merel Dalebout, then a Ph.D. candidate at the University of Auckland in New Zealand, suspected that the whales that had stranded in California weren't really Hector's. At the suggestion of her professor, she contacted biologist James Mead of the Smithsonian Institution in Washington, D.C.

Dr. Mead, curator of marine mammals, keeps a very special collection at the

Rebecca Pugh, research biologist, removes frozen tissue samples from a liquid nitrogen vapor freezer at the Marine Environmental Specimen Bank in Charleston, South Carolina.

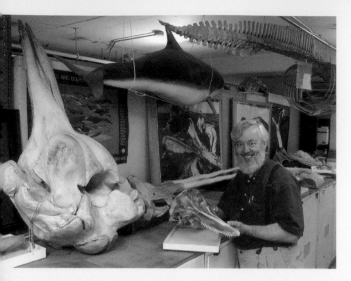

Dr. James Mead, the curator of the marine mammal collection housed at the Smithsonian Institution in Washington, D.C., oversees a collection of tissues and specimens, such as these cetacean skulls and skeletons, that are indispensable to whale scientists around the world.

Whale biologist and DNA expert Merel Dalebout drills into a jawbone of a Cuvier's beaked whale at the University of Haifa, Israel, to get bone powder for DNA extraction. Her research led to the discovery of a new whale species.

Smithsonian. Generally known to the American public as a set of great museums, the Smithsonian also houses the world's most extensive collection of biological specimens, from whale skeletons to tiny worms. Some are in jars, some are in drawers, and others, the whale skulls, are strapped onto metal dollies. Among them are several holotype specimens, which are the standard example of what an individual of a certain species looks like.

Dr. Mead is the world's leading expert on beaked whales. He had identified the 1975 whales as Hector's, although he suspected that they were a new species. At that time, DNA sequencing was only beginning to be used; most of the time, scientists had only the animal's physical appearance and structure to use in determining species. From an examination of these features, Dr. Mead couldn't say for certain that the stranded whales were *not* Hector's beaked whales, so he identified them as such.

By 2002 things had changed; Dalebout had the ability to sequence the DNA of the stranded whales, using the tissues that had been saved. As part of a large project to catalog whale DNA, she compared the DNA of the whales that had stranded in California with DNA from known specimens of Hector's from New Zealand. And she discovered something amazing: the whales that had stranded in California were not Hector's beaked whales. In fact, they were a new species of whale altogether! Called Perrin's beaked whale (*Mesoplodon perrini*), the species became the twenty-first member of the Mesoplodon beaked whales.

Secrets of the ear

Studying whales that have stranded and died helps scientists understand and identify living whales. It may also help save other whales. One of the rarest of all cetaceans is the North Atlantic right whale. Only about three hundred still survive in the entire world. When one dies, its loss has huge implications for the survival of the whole species. Unfortunately, these whales are often struck and killed by fast-moving oceangoing ships. The question is, why?

For the past twenty years, the ears of many stranded North Atlantic right whales have gone to one scientist: Dr. Darlene Ketten of the Woods Hole Oceanographic Institution in Massachusetts. "We have a rather unique collection in my laboratory," she says, "about fifteen right whale ears collected over the years from strandings—not all of them what you would call 'splendid' based on looks (or smell) alone. Some are downright foul, but every one of them is in its own way quite beautiful. They are literally invaluable for research." Dr. Ketten and her associates are trying to find out how hearing works in marine mammals and how these animals use the information they get from sound. In her work, she uses computerized tomography (CT) scanning technology to get a three-dimensional picture of the ears' structure.

Darlene Ketten of the Woods Hole Oceanographic Institution in Massachusetts examines scans of a cetacean's head. By examining cetacean heads and ears, she hopes to learn how endangered North Atlantic right whales hear.

Why study ears?

"The principal reason whale ears are worth investigating is . . . Ginger Rogers," says Dr. Ketten. She explains: "Ginger Rogers and Fred Astaire were a famous dance team. Mr. Astaire was renowned for his grace and agility. What people rarely note is that Ms. Rogers not only matched her partner step for step, she did it wearing a cumbersome gown, in high heels, and backwards. Just as Ginger kept pace with Fred but in a different orientation and with added burdens, whales hear as well as land mammals but in water, a very different medium than air that has special acoustic burdens."

Because they are strictly water animals, cetaceans have a different way of gathering sound than land animals do. For land mammals, like people, sound vibrations travel through the air and enter the ear through a tube called the external ear canal. When a land mammal goes underwater, the ear canal fills up with water, diminishing the animal's ability to hear.

Instead of collecting sound through open ear canals, the toothed whales collect sound through fats near their jaw. At the rear of a whale's jaw are thick pads of fat. These fat pads transmit vibrations in the water to the whale's middle and inner ear. How baleen whales (including the right whale) hear is more of a mystery. Their ear structures differ from those of toothed whales. Some scientists think that sound is transmitted through the skull bones that surround the ear. Others think that baleen whales have more complex soft tissue routes that differ from but are parallel to those of the toothed whales.

By examining cetaceans' heads and ears, Dr. Ketten and her associates hope to learn more about how whales, specifically right whales, hear. "What we're seeing with ship strikes is a pattern of impact coming from the back or side of a whale, not generally head-on. This pattern brings up a good question: Do right whales hear vessels coming?" Understanding the whales' hearing would allow scientists to develop a device that would effectively warn them of approaching vessels. Because so few North Atlantic right whales remain, answering this question is vital if it will help save more right whales from being hit and killed by ships and stave off extinction a little longer.

Analyzing the body tissues of stranded whales and examining their bodies in detail have taught scientists a great deal. They are beginning to understand how well whales have become suited to their watery environment. They are learning about how human activities are affecting the oceans. Often, these lessons are learned from dead animals. However, a more wonderful learning opportunity takes place when a whale strands itself alive and humans get the chance to help it recover and return to the sea.

We have learned a lot from whales that have stranded. Their skeletons are sometimes cleaned, mounted, and used to educate the public, such as this one outside the Seymour Marine Discovery Center of the University of California–Santa Cruz. This skeleton came from a eighty-seven-foot-long female blue whale, who was estimated to be about eighty years old. It is the largest whale skeleton on display in the world.

*The staff of the Cape Cod Stranding Network patrols
seven hundred miles of coastline for strandings.*

A TRAGEDY AND A TRIUMPH

Fortunately, becoming stranded is not an automatic death sentence for cetaceans. Around the world, groups made up of scientists and volunteers respond to strandings and try to save as many animals as possible.

The Cape Cod Stranding Network is an active rescue group in the United States. CCSN director Katie Touhey, a biologist, and her staff patrol seven hundred miles of coastline in Massachusetts for stranded marine animals. In addition, people alert her by cell phone, night, day, weekends, and holidays—it doesn't matter. In 2002, one of CCSN's busiest years, Touhey and her team responded to 296 strandings, including a mass stranding.

In July 2002, sixty pilot whales littered the sand of a Cape Cod beach, as if some giant who'd been playing pick-up sticks had flung them down there. They were of all ages and sizes. Some lay alone; others were stacked on top of one another like pieces of wood. "It was overwhelming, there were so many animals," Touhey recalls.

But she didn't have to handle them all herself: members of the Humane Society of the United States and the International Fund for Animals, CCSN volunteers, and more than a thousand other people had already started helping by covering the whales with damp towels and beach blankets to protect their skin,

Rescuers from the Cape Cod Stranding Network take a blood sample from a stranded whale. Analysis of the blood will give rescuers insight into how well the whale's body is functioning.

and by forming a bucket brigade to keep the whales wet and cool. Yet without water's support, the whales' own weight was killing them slowly; inside their bodies, blood vessels were crushed, cutting off blood flow to vital organs.

After getting organized, Touhey and several others with medical training looked at each whale to evaluate its physical condition. They looked for cuts and lesions. They opened the whales' mouths and peered at the color of their gums—pale gums mean the whale is in shock and that it is very ill. They also watched for foamy green feces, a sign that a whale's gastrointestinal system is beginning to fail. "It's an indication that the whale's chances are not good," Touhey explains. As they checked each animal, Touhey and her team attached a tag to its dorsal fin. The tags allow rescuers to tell the whales apart.

Giving care was complicated by the whales' positioning on top of one another. The whales on top were crushing their fellows below. Working in teams, rescuers nudged the whales on top onto stretchers, then lowered them to the ground. Although the whales were ill, they were still strong—far stronger than the people trying to help. A thrashing tail could easily smash the leg of a well-meaning but unwary rescuer.

Touhey knew that transporting the whales to the water was out of the question. They were too big and too numerous. The tide was low, and the water line was almost a mile away. All the rescuers could do was wait for the tide to return. When it did, they arranged themselves in a long line between the shore and the whales and walked seaward, urging as many whales as possible back out to sea. Yet Touhey was doubtful. Although stranded whales are often refloated, they sometimes strand again, especially if they had been part of a larger group that stranded earlier.

The next day, the news was bad. The whales that had been urged out to sea with the returned tide had stranded once again. Many were already dead

Volunteers and rescuers stand between the shore and the pilot whales, forming a human fence to prevent them from stranding again.

on the sand. Others had no chance of survival. Authorized veterinarians put the suffering whales down, a process called euthanasia. The necessary necropsies were completed and paperwork done. Then the whales were towed out to sea one last time, and their bodies sunk to the depths below. In spite of tremendous effort, all sixty of the whales that had stranded died.

Even if a whale doesn't strand again after being refloated, there's no way to know whether it survived its ordeal. It may die at sea from internal injuries or stress caused by stranding; no one can know for sure. However, some stranded whales are too young to be sent back to sea without the support and care of a pod. Other whales have illnesses that can be cured with human expertise. For whales such as these, there's an alternative beyond refloating or euthanasia: rehabilitation.

In June 1999, two pilot whales were found trapped in the heavy surf on the beach near Chatham, Massachusetts. Katie Touhey and her team responded, and quickly realized that the whales couldn't be safely refloated; they were too young to survive without a pod, and one seemed ill. They needed to go to a rehabilitation center. The best chance the whales had was to go to the Mystic Aquarium in Mystic, Connecticut. It was the only aquarium in New England that could handle two such large patients.

Rescuers loaded the whales into the back of a large rental van, packing ice

Rescued together, these young pilot whales seemed to help each other recover from illness and the stress of being stranded. They recovered faster than whales that had been alone during recovery.

around their bodies to protect them from overheating. The trip from the Cape to Mystic took three hours in the summer heat.

At Mystic, many helping hands—as well as a crane—awaited their arrival. First, rescuers took the larger whale out of the van. At ten feet long, he was about two-thirds the size of an adult whale, and weighed about 850 pounds. He lay still and silent during his physical, not even twitching when aquarium staff used long cotton swabs in his blowhole to take samples of the microbes there.

Placed in a sling hung from a crane, the whale was carefully moved to the aquarium's 100,000-gallon tank (filled with about four feet of water), where he swam without help—a good sign that he was healthy, despite the scrapes and scratches he'd gotten from being tossed about in the Cape Cod surf.

The second whale was smaller, about eight and a half feet long and about six hundred pounds. His physical examination later revealed that he had an infection. Could the bigger whale have been staying with the smaller, sick whale as a protector or friend?

When the smaller whale was moved into the pool, the larger one came over to join him. Throughout their stay, they stayed very close together, touching almost all the time. Scientists have long recognized that pilot whales are one of the most social of all cetaceans, living and traveling in groups of dozens of animals of all ages. But the scientists at the aquarium noticed something remarkable about these two whales: being together actually seemed to help them get better faster.

During their three-month stay at the facility's Aquatic Animal Study Center, the whales gradually returned to health. The smaller whale gained weight—an amazing four hundred pounds!—and reached what is considered a normal size for a whale of his age. The two companions were also more playful than other cetaceans that the Mystic staff had cared for. They leaped out of the water, splashing onlookers, and waved their flippers above the water as they swam on their backs. Despite their best efforts to stay disconnected from the whales, staff and volunteers alike became fond of 25 and 26, as they came to be called.

Researchers knew that both whales were good candidates for release. They didn't have any physical problems that would make survival in the wild difficult. They had learned to hunt for their own food before they had stranded. Most of all, they had each another—a miniature pod of their very own!

And so, the release was planned. The scientists in charge of the release scouted by air for a likely spot and decided on a place southeast of Long Island, where pilot whales had been seen by aerial surveys.

Nature, however, had other ideas. As the release day approached, a hurricane blew up the coast. If the storm-tossed seas were too rough, there would be no chance of releasing 25 and 26. Mystic staff moved up the date, hoping to beat the storm.

The day of the release was rainy and cold, a dismal New England November morning. The first members of the team arrived at the aquarium at 1:30 a.m. to start draining the whales' pool. By 3:00 a.m., the rest of the team had arrived. Their second job in the predawn dark: get the whales out of the pool and into specially made wet transport boxes. These water-tight boxes would hold the whales in slings, partially supported by water. Together, box, whale, and water weighed about ten thousand pounds.

Very early in the morning, aquarium staff members begin to encircle the pilot whales called 25 and 26. They separated the whales and placed each one into a specially constructed sling (rear). A crane hoisted each sling out of the tank and placed it carefully into a wet transport box for the journey home to the sea.

A satellite tag similar to this was attached to each young whale's dorsal fin before they were released. It recorded their movement and diving activity for four months, giving scientists a glimpse into the whales' world.

Next stop: the dock, where the R/V *Connecticut* waited, on loan from the University of Connecticut. The whales and their boxes were carefully moved onto the waiting ship, and the ship set off.

The sky and the sea were both gray. The plan was to carry 25 and 26 out past the tip of Long Island and release them into the Atlantic. Rough seas made the going slow, and the ship's movement rocked the whales in their slings. Would their skin be scraped raw, or would they be injured even more seriously? If they were released closer to shore, would they find and join the whales that had been seen earlier from the air?

Accidental injury was not a risk the aquarium team was willing to take. About eight miles off of Long Island, the captain cut the engines. Working in concert, aquarium staffers opened the front ends of the boxes, pouring gallons of water out over the stern and into the ocean below. Team members counted: "One, two, three!" and pushed with all their strength. The whales' foreheads, and then the rest of their heads, appeared. When they saw each other, they began to whistle and chirp. A few more pushes and they splashed into the sea.

Before the whales returned to the sea, though, aquarium scientists made sure they would "phone home" to Mystic. Scientists attached satellite tags to the whales' dorsal fins. Each time the whales surfaced, the tags sent a signal to an orbiting satellite, which transmitted information on the whales' activities and position to computers at the aquarium. What scientists learned gave them a new look at the world of the whale. Although pilot whales are common, scientists know relatively little about the lives they lead at sea. Over the course of four months, 25 and 26 traveled more than a thousand miles in the Gulf of Maine. They dove to depths of more than a thousand feet—far beyond where light can reach. They stayed underwater for more than twenty-six minutes at a time. And most remarkable of all, the satellite information showed that the two whales were still together.

What lies ahead?

The information from 25 and 26, as well as data collected from other successfully rehabilitated animals, gave whale scientists a tantalizing glimpse into a world humans can only visit. As human understanding of whales has grown, perceptions have changed from those of the days when we saw whales only when they stranded. People no longer see a whale stranding as a windfall that provides meat for food. Fewer and fewer nations accept the view that the whales are in the sea for us to kill. In April 2006, the second-largest Japanese seafood company announced that it was no longer going to hunt whales and sell whale meat to the public, owing to public pressure. Yet the debate over whaling continues.

Over the last few decades, whale scientists have learned much about cetaceans. They have discovered that whales can craft songs, communicate in dialects, and even use tools. They have seen dolphins use sponges to protect their snouts as they looked for prey in the sand; such tool use was once thought to be a skill unique to primates. Yet many questions remain. What are whales' lives like in the sea? How are their societies set up? Can we learn to communicate with them? If so, could we one day explore the sea with them? What do they think about?

Won't it be interesting to find out?

Is it a jump for joy, a way to communicate, or just an attempt to knock off whale lice? Future scientists may find out exactly why humpback whales breach like this, leaping out of the water and crashing back with a tremendous splash.

ACKNOWLEDGMENTS AND THANKS

A book is never an individual effort. I wish to thank the following people for taking time out of their days to help me by providing information or images, or for pointing me in the right direction to find that information and those images. I particularly want to thank my family for their patience with the writer in the house.

This list is in no particular order, and I ask forgiveness from anyone I've missed:

Ann Rider, Arnold Miller, Carl Buell, Hans Thewissen, James Mead, British Divers Marine Life Rescue, Darlene Ketten, Katie Touhey and Sarah Herzig, Cameron McPherson, Catherine Hill Fay and Richard Fay, Whitlow Au, Katherine Zecca, Kathy Black, Gabrielle Durham, Kathy Squires, Keith Chandler, Don Hurlbert, Ruth Williams, Sasha Blanton, Art Ciccone, Cindy Driscoll, Glenn Evans, Don Kenny, Geoff Hook, Rebecca Pugh, Iain Kerr, Toni Rosenberg, and Alison Kerr Miller.

SOURCES

Barnett, James. Evaluation of rehabilitation as an option for stranded dolphins, porpoises, and whales. Winston Churchill Memorial Trust Travel Fellowship, 2002. (Accessed at www.bdmlr.org.uk, March 23, 2005.)

Benders, F.P.A., S. P. Beerens, and W. C. Verboom. "SAKAMATA: A tool to avoid whale strandings." *Proceedings of the European Conference on Undersea Defence Technology,* UDT Europe 2004, June 22–25, Nice, France.

British Divers Marine Life Rescue. *Marine Mammal Medic Handbook.* www. bdmlr.org.uk (accessed March 23, 2005).

Chadwick, Douglas. Evolution of whales: Strange route to the sea. *National Geographic* (November 2001): 64–77.

Chivers, Susan J. "Cetacean Life History." In *Encyclopedia of Marine Mammals,* edited by William F. Perrin, Bernd Würsig, and J.G.M. Thewissen, 221–25. San Diego: Academic Press, 2002.

Clapham, Phillip J. "Whaling, Modern." In *Encyclopedia of Marine Mammals,* edited by William F. Perrin, Bernd Würsig, and J.G.M. Thewissen, 1328–32. San Diego: Academic Press, 2002.

Cowan, Daniel F. "Pathology." In *Encyclopedia of Marine Mammals,* edited by William F. Perrin, Bernd Würsig, and J.G.M. Thewissen, 883–90. San Diego: Academic Press, 2002.

Dunn, J. Lawrence, John D. Buck, and Todd R. Robeck. "Bacterial Diseases of Cetaceans and Pinnipeds." In *CRC Handbook of Marine Mammal Medicine,* 2nd ed., edited by Leslie A. Dierauf and Frances M. D. Gulland, 309–35. Boca Raton, Fla.: CRC Press, 2001.

Ellis, Richard. *Men and Whales,* 33–71, 131–40. New York: Lyons Press, 1999.

———. "Whaling, Traditional." In *Encyclopedia of Marine Mammals,* edited by William F. Perrin, Bernd Würsig, and J.G.M. Thewissen, 1316–28. San Diego: Academic Press, 2002.

Environmental Protection Agency (EPA) 2003. Ambient aquatic life water quality criteria for tributyltin. Available through the National Technical Information Service, 5285 Port-Royal Rd., Springfield, VA 21161, and at www. epa.gov/waterscience/criteria/tributyltin.

Fordyce, R. Ewan. "Cetacean Evolution." In *Encyclopedia of Marine Mammals,* edited by William F. Perrin, Bernd Würsig, and J.G.M. Thewissen, 214–20. San Diego: Academic Press, 2002.

Forstell, Paul H. "Popular Culture and Literature." In *Encyclopedia of Marine Mammals,* edited by William F. Perrin, Bernd Würsig, and J.G.M. Thewissen, 957–74. San Diego: Academic Press, 2002.

Grzimek, Bernhard. *Grzimek's Animal Life Encyclopedia*, 2nd ed., vol. 15, *Cetacea,* 1–11.

Gulland, Frances M. D., Leslie A. Dierauf, and Teri K. Rowles. "Marine Mammal Stranding Networks." In *CRC Handbook of Marine Mammal Medicine,* 2nd ed., edited by Leslie A. Dierauf and Frances M. D. Gulland, 45–66. Boca Raton, Fla.: CRC Press, 2001.

"Harpoons and Other Whalecraft." New Bedford Whaling Museum Web site. (Accessed July 13, 2005. www.whalingmuseum.org/kendall/whalecraft/whalecraft_index.html.)

Hunter, Robert, and Rex Weyler. *To Save a Whale: The Voyages of Greenpeace.* San Francisco: Chronicle Books, 1978.

International Whaling Commission (IWC) Member Countries and Commissioners. IWC Web site www.iwcoffice.org/commission/members.html (accessed July 12, 2005).

"Introduction to the Cetacea." www.ucmp.berkeley.edu/mammal/cetacea/cetacean.html.

Kennedy-Stoskopf, Suzanne. "Viral Diseases." In *CRC Handbook of Marine Mammal Medicine,* 2nd ed., edited by Leslie A. Dierauf and Frances M. D. Gulland, 285–307. Boca Raton, Fla.: CRC Press, 2001.

Ketten, Darlene R. "Cetacean Ears." In *Hearing by Whales and Dolphins,* edited by Whitlow W. L. Au, Arthur N. Popper, and Richard R. Fay, 43–108. New York: Springer-Verlag, 2000.

———. Right whales' ears. Paper presented at the North Atlantic Right Whale Forum. Archived on the Woods Hole Oceanographic Institution Ocean Life Institute Web site, www.whoi.org.

Klinowska, M. Cetacean live stranding dates relate to geomagnetic disturbances. In *Aquatic Mammals,* 1986, 11–13, 109 19.

———. Cetacean live stranding sites relate to geomagnetic topography. In *Aquatic Mammals,* 1985, 1–1, 27–32.

Krischvnik, J. L., Andrew E. Dizon, and James A. Westphal. Evidence from strandings for geomagnetic sensitivity in cetaceans. *Journal of Experimental Biology* 120 (1986): 1–24.

Krischvnik, J. L., Michael M. Walker, and Carol E. Diebel. Magentite-based magentoreception. *Current Opinion in Neurobiology* 11 (2001): 426–67.

Lei Song, Achim Seeger, and Joseph Santos-Sacchi. On membrane motor activity and chloride flux in the outer hair cell: Lessons learned from the environmental toxin tributylin. *Biophysical Journal BioFAST,* published on December 13, 2004, as dol: 10.1529/biophysj.104.053579.

MacLean, Stephen A., Glenn W. Sheehan, and Anne M. Jensen. "Inuit and Marine Mammals." In *Encyclopedia of Marine Mammals,* edited by William F. Perrin, Bernd Würsig, and J.G.M. Thewissen, 641–52. San Diego: Academic Press, 2002.

McNally, Robert. *So Remorseless a Havoc: Of Dolphins, Whales, and Men.* Boston: Little, Brown, 1981.

Mooney, Nick. *Action Plan for Whale Rescues: Tasmania.* From the Wildlife Section, Nature Conservation Branch, Division of Resource Management and Conservation, Department of Primary Industries, Water, and Environment, Hobart, Tasmania, Australia.

Murphy, Jim. *Gone A-Whaling: The Lure of the Sea and the Hunt for the Great Whale*, 9–33, 151–81. Boston: Houghton Mifflin, 2004.

National Research Council of the National Academies. *Ocean Noise and Marine Mammals,* 2nd ed. Washington, D.C.: National Academy of Sciences, 2004.

"Overview of American Whaling." New Bedford Whaling Museum Web site (accessed July 13, 2005). www.whalingmuseum.org/kendall/index_KI.html.

Perrin, William, and Joseph R. Geraci. "Stranding." In *Encyclopedia of Marine Mammals,* edited by William F. Perrin, Bernd

Würsig, and J.G.M. Thewissen, 1192–97. San Diego: Academic Press, 2002.

Rowles, Teri K., Frances M. Van Dolah, and Aleta A. Hohn. "Gross Necropsy and Specimen Collection Protocols." In *CRC Handbook of Marine Mammal Medicine,* 2nd ed., edited by Leslie A. Dierauf and Frances M. D. Gulland, 449–70. Boca Raton, Fla.: CRC Press, 2001.

St. Aubin, David J., and Leslie A. Dierauf. "Stress and Marine Mammals." In *CRC Handbook of Marine Mammal Medicine,* 2nd ed., edited by Leslie A. Dierauf and Frances M. D. Gulland, 253–69. Boca Raton, Fla.: CRC Press, 2001.

Thewissen, Hans. "Hearing Research." www.darla.neoucom.edu/DEPTS/ANAT/Thewissen/whale_origins/os/hearing.html.

Touhey, Katie. Personal communication.

Walker, Michael M., Todd E. Dennis, and Joseph L. Kirschvink. The magnetic sense and its use in long-distance navigation by animals. *Current Opinion in Neurobiology* 12 (2002): 735–44.

Walker, Michael M., Joseph L. Kirschvink, Gufran Ahmed, and Andrew E. Diction. Evidence that fin whales respond to the geomagnetic field during migration. *Journal of Experimental Biology* 171 (1992): 67–78.

Walsh, Michael T., Ruth Y. Ewing, Daniel K. Odell, and Gregory D. Bossart. "Mass Strandings of Cetaceans." In *CRC Handbook of Marine Mammal Medicine,* 2nd ed., edited by Leslie A. Dierauf and Frances M. D. Gulland, 83–95. Boca Raton, Fla.: CRC Press, 2001.

Wartzok, Douglas, and Darlene R. Ketten. "Marine Mammal Sensory Systems." In *Biology of Marine Mammals,* edited by John E. Reynolds III and Sentiel A. Rommel, 117–75. Washington, D.C.: Smithsonian Institution Press, 1999.

Wells, Randall S., Daryl J. Boness, and Galen B. Rathburn. "Behavior." In *Biology of Marine Mammals,* edited by John E. Reynolds III and Sentiel A. Rommel, 324–422. Washington, D.C.: Smithsonian Institution Press, 1999.

"Whaling." In *Encyclopaedia Britannica.* From Encyclopedia Britannica Premium Service. www.britannica.com/ed/article?tocld=225363 (accessed March 5, 2005).

Whitehead, Hal. "Sperm Whale, *Physeter macrocephalus.*" In *Encyclopedia of Marine Mammals,* edited by William F. Perrin, Bernd Würsig, and J.G.M. Thewissen, 1165–72. San Diego: Academic Press, 2002.

Young, Nina M., and Sara L. Shapiro. "U.S. Federal Legislation Governing Marine Mammals." In *CRC Handbook of Marine Mammal Medicine,* 2nd ed., edited by Leslie A. Dierauf and Frances M. D. Gulland, 741–66. Boca Raton, Fla.: CRC Press, 2001.

acoustic: having to do with sound.

adaptation: a physical or behavioral feature of an animal or plant that helps it survive.

bacterium: a single-celled organism; most are not harmful.

baleen: fibrous plates that hang from the upper jaw of mysticete whales and act as strainers, holding prey animals in when the whale forces water out of its mouth.

baleen whales: whales that have fibrous plates of baleen hanging from their upper jaws; the baleen whales include the blue whale, fin whale, and humpback whale.

beaked whales: medium-size whales that have prominent snouts, or beaks; males very often have oversize teeth in the lower jaw.

behavior: a way of responding to something that occurs in the environment.

beluga: a relatively small, white toothed whale that lives in the Arctic.

blowhole: a cetacean's nostril, located on top of its head.

blubber: a layer of fat beneath a whale's skin that provides insulation against the cold.

blue whale: the largest whale, and the largest animal known to have ever lived on Earth.

bottlenose dolphin: a frequently studied species of dolphin found worldwide in tropical and temperate waters, including the Pacific and Atlantic Oceans; it is light gray, with a prominent beak.

bowhead: a large black baleen whale that lives in the Arctic; sometimes called the Greenland right whale.

case: the capsule inside a sperm whale's head that contains fatty oil and is believed to play a role in echolocation.

cetaceans: whales, dolphins, and porpoises, the group of marine mammals that belong to the order *Cetacea*.

coast: land bordering the sea.

cochlea: a spiral-shaped organ inside the ear, which is lined with hair cells; pressure changes in cochlear fluid inside the cochlea are changed to nerve impulses.

commercial whaling: the hunting of whales to make money from the sale of parts taken from their bodies, such as meat and baleen.

DNA: deoxyribonucleic acid, a molecule present in every cell of the body that contains the unique directions for making that particular kind of living thing.

ear canal: the tube that connects the outside world with the eardrum so sound vibrations can travel into the middle ear.

echolocation: a process by which a toothed whale sends out sound impulses, which travel through the water and then back after they bounce off an object or obstacle.

endangered: describes an animal or plant species with very few remaining members; an endangered animal is in danger of becoming extinct.

Endangered Species Act: U.S. law that prohibits people from teasing, killing, or taking from the wild any members of a species in danger of becoming extinct.

esophagus: the muscular tube that leads from the mouth to the stomach.

euthanasia: humane killing by an injection of a drug such as phenobarbital.

extinct: said of an animal or plant species with no more living members; for example, the passenger pigeon.

factory ship: the largest ship in a whaling fleet, where the whales are cut up.

flipper: one of two appendages in the lower front of a cetacean's body; also called dorsal fins, flippers are used in steering and are roughly equivalent to human arms.

fluke: either of two tail fins of a cetacean.

forceps: tweezers.

fossil: the naturally preserved remains or traces of an animal or plant that lived long ago.

habitat: the place in which an animal or plant lives.

harbor porpoise: a small species of porpoise.

harpoon: a pointed, barbed spear used to kill whales.

humpback whale: a baleen whale characterized by extremely long dorsal fins and elaborate, beautiful songs.

International Whaling Commission: the group that sets rules for countries that conduct whaling.

lesion: a damaged area in a tissue or organ.

lymph nodes: roundish lumps in the body system that carries white blood cells and filters bacteria from the blood.

magnetic field: generated by the movement of the earth's core, this invisible series of lines of magnetic energy surrounds Earth.

Marine Mammal Protection Act: U.S. law that prevents people from teasing, killing, or taking from the wild any cetacean, seal, sea lion, sea otter, or polar bear, all classified as marine mammals.

mass stranding: the coming ashore of a group of cetaceans, after which they become stuck on land.

migration route: a path that an animal regularly follows as it moves from one place to another; for example, to bear young or to find food.

minke whale: the smallest rorqual whale.

mysticetes: the group of whales that have their upper jaw fringed with baleen.

necropsy: a physical examination of a dead whale or other animal, which includes dissecting the body, removing and studying certain organs, and taking samples of tissues.

North Atlantic right whale: a seriously endangered whale; as of 2006, approximately three hundred were believed to survive.

nutrient: a substance, such as protein, that provides nourishment.

oceanographer: a scientist who specializes in studying the ocean and its life forms.

odontocetes: the toothed whales.

paleontologist: a scientist who specializes in studying fossil organisms.

parasite: an organism that lives on or inside another organism, taking from this organism the food it needs to survive.

pathologist: a scientist who specializes in the causes of diseases.

pilot whale: two species, the short-finned and the long-finned, which are both relatively common and are found in family groups.

pneumonia: an illness of the lungs in which the air sacs fill with pus.

pod: a group, or herd, of whales.

poison: a substance that can harm or kill if enough of it is taken into the body.

predator: an animal that eats other animals in order to survive.

psychologist: a person who studies how people or nonhuman animals behave.

quota: a limit, usually given as a particular number.

refloated: said of a cetacean that is pushed back out to sea after a stranding.

rehabilitation: the process of returning a stranded cetacean to health in an animal-care facility, such as an aquarium.

rorqual: one of the sleek, fast-moving species of baleen whales, such as the blue, fin, minke, or sei.

sanctuary: a place of safety.

solar flares: eruptions of extremely hot gases from the sun's surface.

sonar: a process by which a ship or submarine sends out sound impulses, which travel through the water and then back after they bounce off an object or obstacle.

Soviet Union: the former federation of Communist nations that dissolved in 1991.

species: a group of living things made up of organisms that are similar to one another and capable of producing offspring.

sperm whale: the largest of the toothed whales.

spermaceti: a waxy substance found inside a large capsule in the head of a sperm whale (or a bottlenosed whale), which may play a role in focusing the sounds the whales make in echolocation.

steam engine: an engine that produces power when a burning fuel, such as coal or wood, heats water in a large container called a boiler, and the steam that results passes through a turbine, a fanlike arrangement of blades, which spins and generates power.

steamship: a ship powered by a steam-driven engine.

strand (cetaceans): to come ashore, as a result of natural causes or human activity, and become stuck on land.

stranding: the coming ashore of cetaceans, after which they become stuck on land.

streamlined: shaped so as to move easily through the air or the water; sleek.

stress: a physical and emotional reaction to demands put on a living thing by its environment; a little stress is normal, but too much can lead to illness.

tallow: animal fat.

theory: a scientific, evidence-based idea that is an explanation for a phenomenon observed in nature.

tissue: a group of similar cells that share a certain job in the body.

toothed whales: whales that have teeth in their jaws, including the orca, sperm whale, and dolphins and porpoises.

toxins: poisons.

tried: boiled in huge vats.

Vikings: seagoing traders and raiders from the Scandinavian nations who sailed from the eighth through the eleventh century.

virus: a microscopic object that causes disease by infecting healthy cells and using them to reproduce; viruses are not usually considered living things.

whale oil: a fatty liquid obtained by boiling down whale blubber, bones, and flesh.

whalebone: another word for baleen, which is not really bone.

whaling: the hunting of whales for food, oil, and other commercial products.

zero quota: a limit to hunting that prohibits the killing of any animals at all.

Zodiac: a brand of small, fast, inflatable rubber boats, powered by outboard engines.

Other books you might enjoy in the Scientists in the Field series

"This series has done much to expand the horizons of young readers who think that science can only be done in laboratories." —*Kirkus Reviews*

"Consistently excellent." —*Booklist*

Tracking Trash: Flotsam, Jetsam, and the Science of Ocean Motion by Loree Griffin Burns

Quest for the Tree Kangaroo: An Expedition to the Cloud Forest of New Guinea by Sy Montgomery, photographs by Nic Bishop

Diving to a Deep-Sea Volcano by Kenneth Mallory

The Prairie Builders: Reconstructing America's Lost Grasslands by Sneed B. Collard III

Gorilla Doctors: Saving Endangered Great Apes by Pamela Turner

The Tarantula Scientist by Sy Montgomery, photographs by Nic Bishop

The Woods Scientist by Stephen R. Swinburne, photographs by Susan C. Morse

Looking for Life in the Universe by Ellen Jackson, photographs by Nic Bishop

Secrets of Sound: Studying the Calls of Whales, Elephants, and Birds by April Pulley Sayre

Project Ultraswan by Elinor Osborn

The Bug Scientists by Donna Jackson

The Snake Scientist by Sy Montgomery, photographs by Nic Bishop

Hidden Worlds: Looking Through a Scientist's Microscope by Stephen Kramer, photographs by Dennis Kunkel

Swimming with Hammerhead Sharks by Kenneth Mallory

Anthropologist: Scientist of the People by Mary Batten, photographs by A. Magdalena Hurtado and Kim Hill

Digging for Bird-Dinosaurs by Nic Bishop

The Wildlife Detectives by Donna Jackson, photographs by Wendy Shattil and Bob Rozinski

Once a Wolf by Stephen R. Swinburne, photographs by Jim Brandenburg